THE SPILLED INK OF TIME

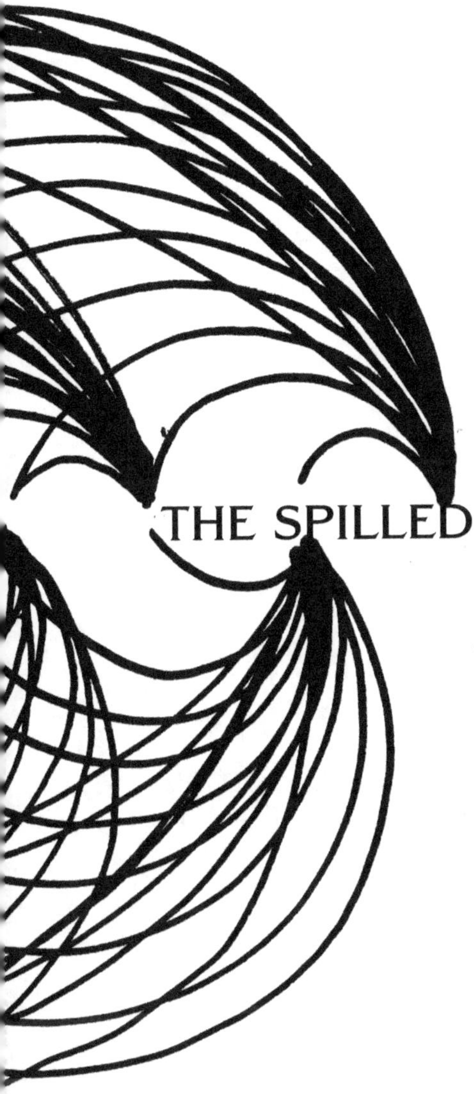

THE SPILLED INK OF TIME

Jonas Zdanys

ISBN: 979-8-9858194-2-7

The Spilled Ink of Time was published in Brooklyn, New York by Black Spruce Press, on February 16, 2024.

Images by Steven Schroeder: cover "pizzicato on crystal clouds", acrylic on hardboard, 2022; title page adapted from "Beat of The Sounding Body" study, 2020

The book is set in Grand Central & 11/13 LTC Kennerly Pro.

Design by forgetgutenberg.

Acknowledgements:
Parts of some of these pieces appeared as experimental unfinished and untitled outlines and notes in *Notebook Sketches*. "The Woman on the Bridge" appeared as a limited edition chapbook. "The Angels of Wine" appeared in the University of Georgia Press' anthology *The Poetry of Men's Lives* edited by Al Zolynas and Fred Moramarco and, in a different version, in the numbered limited edition, *Lithuanian Crossing*. "The Word" and "The Things of the Eye" appeared, in different versions, in the numbered limited edition, *Lithuanian Crossing*.

Contents

How I Named Myself

My parents died before I was born,
so I invented myself
just as I invented them,
It was reason enough to be resentful,
a sensible response
to a series of candid snapshots scattered in a kitchen drawer
that weigh everything down with a sad ring as the lights cut
a frail path that rouses the lucid air.
I chose the wind to fall with me,
the close of day half-buried
in the back of death's particular stop, coaxing the pale tones
of consolation from the incorrigible stars.
It was a dead giveaway, a measured pattern
that traces truth on sibilant water,
the flame that roots in its buried keel and consumes itself
The pendulum of day marks its desolate hour.
The mirror that held their thin reflections breaks
as it gives mine back to me.

Clinging to the First Beam of light

He woke to the ghosts of wild horses
running down the long road
toward dawn
drifting through old doors that opened
on the other side of the earth,
their dappled hooves singing nothing, singing nothing,
to a random wind.
He doesn't know why the old woman at the window is weeping,
why her hands still cling to the first beam of light.
The ashes on her pillow vanish in the four corners of the room.
The day echoes in hollow dust.
They are wrapped in the drying shudder of black mud.
She curls the pinnacle of heaven.
She rusts the dull brown stones.
The weather changes,
the morning's cold.

His body, undefeated,
slips away underground.
He prays for the dark bells,
for the first lights in the sky,
for a way home.

What Midnight Does at Midnight

Midnight kneels in the park by the river
like a blind child.
No one can hear or see it
and the light that comes
unexpectedly around the corner
is hollow at the core.
It drifts in its own darkness,
scattering to shudders on the windows
and ledges of slow gray houses,
like the remnants of voices on a rising wind.
The secrets of the street whisper
across the thin cut of the moon,
clouds brushing invisible through the dust
of the rooftops and walls.
Ghosts loiter on stone benches.
Cold crouches in the passing bell.
The mute white horse sleeps with eyes open,
swept free and frail in the refuge of dead branches,
one of the shapes of the world
that cast no shadows in the glass.
Its sad bones land soft and low
on the dark street,

The thin light from the last star
at the edge of the galaxy
Hangs in the air like a white old bulb
fluttering on its wire string.

The Angels of Wine

He died before my children were born
and I tell them
about him sometimes,
when I tell our family's stories:
uncle and godfather,
raw-boned and visionary,
alcoholic son
and failed father,
in the end a weak reed
no one leaned upon,
who struggled with his gloom
and self-loathing
and was caught in a trap
he laid for himself
in the teeth of the wind.
He would listen to me in moments of clarity,
drawing a breath as if wanting to speak
and then letting it out in a sigh and waiting for me
to talk myself out.
He would nod when I said that life
is not something that was waiting for us
around the corner but was here and now,
and then would ask me for money
for a bottle of sweet wine,
too tired and shaky
to invent another lie.
It was not for his thirst,
he would say,
but because with it
everything grew remote
and the stars in the sky began to swim
and the horizon expanded again.
Once he said he thought we gave
birth to our death,
like something lifting inside us,
like the tunnel where he thrashed and choked and could not breathe

because there was no light.
That's how they found him early one morning
as the sun touched
the edges of his room:
the artery in his liver spilling his life out
into something scarlet and black,
his nose burrowed between the thighs of the woman
he lived with like a small lost dog
looking for the place he'd come from
and where he wanted to return.
I think of him like that but do not tell my children
the details of his final story:
lying in the dark in a pool of his own blood,
not knowing what was rolling over him
as a veil of grayness
covered his eyes,
perhaps dreaming one last time
of the daughter
he had abandoned
or the grandchildren
he would never see
or the angels
that would come to him
with the wine
in the dead of night.

Wheeling the Old Moon

He takes a deep breath,
pauses by the bent sycamore.
The light is out on the bridge.
White shadows
wheel the old moon.
The city breaks on the marrow.
Time drowns in its own past.
It is the rifting of things.
A transcendent beauty,
The steady mustering of pale clouds,
every detail clear.

The day to come bright, but birdless.

The Woman on the Bridge

1.
It is a long path of scuffed cinders and red stones
curving past the small spaces between white trees.

Up ahead are the ripples and curls of a river
below a gray stone bridge.

Flurries of dust and loose dirt sift
in patterns on the stones of the road.

The horizon hangs low above the
bridge and its brown wooden railings
and posts.

I see her from a distance, dressed in a short
coat and skirt the same colors as the bridge.

She stands at the near end as I approach,
presses her face close, calls me by another's
name.

Something falls from the sky.
Time reassembles itself.

The black flowers at the bottom
of the bridge suddenly blossom.

2.
Night has already fallen.
I light a lamp for her in the shaded
room but she pushes me away.

I adapt without complaint to this new pattern.
I sleep fitfully
and when I wake my hands are cold.

Morning comes tapping at the window,
moves erratically from point to point in
the empty room.

3.
There seems to be time for all things,
time enough for everything,
even for the silence between us.

I rise and follow her across the yard
to the cinder and stone path that leads to the bridge.
I am aware of the vastness of the sky above me.

She holds out her hand to me
offering something, all feathers and bone,
a soul stirring its wings.

On the bridge I have no fear now.
If I fall into the air I know I will float away,
receding, separated, drifting.

If I fall on the bridge I will be a storyteller
who lost the thread of his tale
in the middle of telling it:
a space, a blankness huddled in a tree
that has lost its root.

4.
The hours pass in a flat hard place
without shadow or depth
and time is dry as paper.
This morning I do not know
 if it began or did not begin
or the possibilities of abstraction.

The body grows silent among
the changing echoes
of what was.

The shifting light
of all that has disappeared
beyond the hope of what will be.

Perhaps in time
I will learn
to howl at the moon

watch birds
settle to roost
in light refracted on the bridge

skip over
whole days and nights
as if they did not happen.

Space decomposes and recomposes itself
before my eyes
as I move down the slope to the river.

5.
It was how the story ended:
sand already in the boy's
mouth settling in, claiming him

carrying him
through the shallows
into the darker depths,

part of his essence
not here but in the future
like a shadow cast before him,

the dark haze of hope
he can never catch
as his trembling at last subsides.

A fly settles on his cheek,
cleans itself,
circles and settles again.

6.
She asks me why I live
in the green hills

I smile

I do not
answer
I am completely at peace

a blossom
floats past
on the current below

I tell her
there are worlds beyond this one
among the white stars

7.
A day must have passed,
must have intervened here,
something must have changed,

but I am wary
of such suppositions,
impatient with the flow of time.

Sunlight pours through the window
onto an empty bed.
The door is locked.

I help her undress in
the airless silence
of this place, my heart quickens

as her brown skirt falls to the floor,
a suspension, a moment
before the return of time.
Her body is mapped with the signs
that she is beyond her term,
eternal, thrashing about, transparent

struggling for air
in the faint turbulence of
the time that passes.
the grief of the unanswerable question
spreads over the walls.

8.
It is time for what comes
out of the ashes to come.

Time for that which shows
through the flesh
flesh that extends itself to air

This is how the trap is laid,
how they are caught.

The dry earth soaks up
the blood of its creatures, never sated.

If this is my fate I'd rather be
a broken stick in an empty
field.

On the far side of the bridge
something pale stands out against the sky.

It will be a difficult day,

a day for waiting.

Tomorrow will die by your hand,
the end not yet written,
The ceremony of time
anoints its own indifference.

9.
They have made a room without a window.
I cannot see but I remember how

morning after morning the day
passes, dusk falls, and darkness comes.

Here, someone closes the doors and switches on the lights,
and there are dissatisfied murmurs all around,

discontent at the dissolution of the membrane
between the world and the self inside.

I must have slept. When I opened my eyes
she was kneeling beside me, feeling under the quilt.

For a while I was nowhere, shook my head,
this is my hand, I say, this is the bed, this the floor,

my soul alert, darting, and in the morning
when she reemerged at the edge of my oblivion

swirls of mist floated past her, a dark speck
moving against the stillness of other dark specks,

embraced the bridge and floated
away with the spirits and wraiths,

the great beam of my vision illuminating
the helpless complicity of all who watched,

all they said to one another in this windowless
room in the closest dead of night.

Days and nights wheel past as the lights in the
room brighten to gray-green and then darken to black.

In a week or a month
I will have forgotten everything,

will look around intently and no longer know
who waits for me to step into the shadow.

10.
Heavy rain sheets over the edges
of the roof, swirls of water on the grass
and trees just visible through the window.

The earth returns into itself
and the leaves fall and the stars dip
low in the clouds on the horizon.

I think of you on the bridge, wound
together a thousand times, and feel the
stirring of the air as I call to you in the dark.

This is the grace of things to come,
the one sorrow I walk through in my sleep,
the shine I move toward as the wind shifts.

The rain is the only line drawn between us tonight.
The veil of grayness outside the window grows
lighter. Out ahead, the pale blue of farther skies.

11.
When time drifts like a heavy truth
across the bridge
and the sky comes down
and covers me completely

I am held by nothing and hold onto nothing,
see nothing inside of nothing, sit bewildered
like the man who wondered all his life and discovered and then forgot

the hidden meanings of things
set loose in the landscapes of sheer earth
in moments of no importance
that spill themselves like dry leaves

and move from one stillness to another,
to the indecipherable taste
and bitter dust
of dry seasons kept from decay.

Revelation, intuition, inspiration:
it would be better to be an empty mind,
the dull and dimly lit, than to live
with the weariness of this uncertainty,

to be neither still nor in motion,
neither force nor will, not dream or guess,
but everything at once, the eternal now,
where nothing returns and nothing repeats,

searching for the metaphysics of the spirit
not the small realities of the body,
the swift-colored thing that passes
in canceled desires and the rising of the dead,

not knowing and not keeping,
dissolved to a drift of smoke
as the moon swings dark and away
and the sky withers and the ash falls.

I have considered such things often,
have fallen with the weight of things
everywhere and unobserved,
have understood how it all begins:

at night when the lights come on
and life changes its face
in every crevice and corner,
I see her in the distance on the bridge

breathing the last breath of dusk,
pointing with unmistakable clarity
to what we had come for as the wind
shifts and darkness invades the day.

12.
If there is magic in this world
I'll stand where I'm standing now
here on the dark bridge.

The spirit moves forward
but the body persists
where the winds and waters meet

I stand beside myself
the finite in the infinite
Upon the rock at the white shore

I have seen what I have seen

the mind in the air
the swift tide of longing
the clean tear

The joy of being
the sigh of the soul pale body
and the naked ease of myself

The word made word and flesh
thick waters dropped seed
the blue expression
the whole of light

Where the river lies still
clear night telling who comes and
goes the breath's moment that moved
on

Time folds and the sounds I
hear in this vulnerable place
tell of dust leaves ash idea revelation

13.
We let the day take us where it wants
like a slow shifting of the bridge.

Just beyond the gate
everything stays as it is.

The straight trees the curved
sky the slow falling rain.

Day after day
nothing repeats itself.

The window reflects a chair a lamp
a changing moon.

The end of it all weightless the sky the eye
sees,
the landscapes of the past it cannot find.

The light begins to thin
the light we move toward all dust and colorless
moan.

We are the last to leave after
all the others have left.

We stand on the other side
whispering something.

We hear it gathering around us
disappearing calling us back

To where time peels to its own
negative and is locked in a small
black box.

14.
I dreamed of being lost and covered with leaves.

I woke up shouting, my throat full.
It was night again and I licked the mirror
into which I was staring clean.
White light reflected in shards of glass
on all sides and in a minute all was done.

I have gone over that moment a thousand times,
have thought about it for a thousand moments: it was a
sadness, a pillar of smoke dry as the world
fallen around my neck, a disturbance of the soul,
all lightness gone, the desperate silence of a deserted house,
and I understood that I am the last of my kind,
living in the old way, drifting through time:
even if I lay low and breathe quietly
they'll hear my heart beating: clenching
and unclenching like a stranger's fist in my chest.

I no longer know what to do with my face.

The sun had set, the wind began to bite,
a half moon was coming through the
clouds.
I took the old road, waving my arms,
and heard the green music.

No one is forgotten.
In a moment of astonishment
I tumbled into the cauldron of history

and saw the burned posts of the bridge,
the vast airiness of space between heaven
and the brown lines of the river,
the outlines of the words of love
she mouthed to me soundlessly there.
I felt the shame of private knowledge,
the moral dimension of my plight.

I am drowning,
arguing with cold
clarity for all that is
unheard,
gripping the bars of the gate.

I listened
and nodded
and dreamed,
shivering with cold,
and my fingers
would not
straighten.

Something has fallen on me.
I crept away, touching the silence
of airless places, was pulled this way
and that by the shrunken tug of the moon,
leaped and groaned at the far edges
of the sky, watched patterns
of chaos manifest
themselves
as moments of transfiguration.

I welcomed that dissolution,
pondered its sounds.
Night pushed a stick into my mouth,
left its thin black mark on
everything.

Tomorrow will be a new day.
Tomorrow will not be today.
Today I am so tired that I reel on my
feet, sob from the heart like a frightened
child.

I am hollow:
unthinking, inarticulate, without
imagination:
I come to speak but have nothing to say:
today is the day but today has passed:
how will I know how I lived in this place, in this
time: swept over the brink, a cold wind blowing,
rain falling on barren soil.

An hour must have
passed or the blink of an
eye:
events overtook me:
the spark flickered and lost itself
at once.
 I followed the reflected light,
crystalline and bloodless,
and gripped the ground to steady myself,
to keep myself from spinning off the earth.

The thought began to float away but I clung to it:
there will be another time, and if not, then I don't
mind: I am a blind man dancing, as if in another country,
struggling for a foothold in unfamiliar sand.

All my life I waited for someone to call to in the dark.
I see them. I call out *here* here I am *here*.

They skulk in the open, stand in a circle around
me, don't know what to say or do.

I am, to some of them or to many,
the beast that stares out from behind
the gate or from across the bridge,
a laboring creature, the
obscurest of the obscure, the
begetter of my own existence.
I whisper and tumble free as the odor of
smoke. I stumble and fall, reach out a slow hand,
wince at the sharpness of the light.

The fear of the past day has lost its tense.
I will defend the cause of justice,
the precious safety of the fragile and the liquid-eyed,
will forever shake off the weight
of the resentful gazes that rest on me,

God's time is not our time.
I dream but I don't think
I dream of God
or that God dreams of me.
I dream that there is water everywhere,
paths that lead nowhere:
holy ground:
resurrection from the earth:
the soul emerging, a creature of air:
truth frozen in its tracks, the
future disguised
in the name of some present abstraction.

The wind dropped, the air was clear.
The silence was so dense, there was nowhere to hide,
and the ground sighed as my body returned
not to the great cycle but to the jagged time
of rise and fall, of start and finish, of up and down,
of beginning and end. Time stopped and then started
again. I did not want to be drawn away,
struggling and lost, gesturing
from horizon to horizon in joy or lamentation,

living between reason and truth in a secret life I do
not see or understand,
a spirit invisible,
but the vision faded
and the dust came and the leaves.

15.
Tomorrow
when the war ends
when the moon seeps like dust
through the crack in the door
and draws the fictions of our souls

Tomorrow
when we hang our lives
in the attics of old houses
and fragments of time
are like a knocking on the wall

Tomorrow
when we see dead faces
in the mirror, on the pillow
and feel the brevity of our
days
in the window and the water below

Tomorrow
when we repeat the sounds
of the letters of our names
and touch the thinnest
edge of the voice of God
as it whispers the letters
of our names

Tomorrow
when the haze in me lifts
when every hour is mine
and the song of the infinite

is like a silence of the
heart

I will empty the drawers
undress bathe breathe go out
sketch the anguish of regret
redeem myself feel the pain of separation
complain softly rise up float across the skin of the
earth feel the scales thicken fan my wings
pause stare out into the distance
render myself into words
let go of myself let go of all of you
be stunned astounded free of feeling
be turned to stone see the long night ahead
sleep dream wake wait until tomorrow

16.
That year there was no
spring. After winter came
winter.

The air grows dry and light
by late December as the heaviness of fall
slips away into the last folded corner of
the sky.

The day passes uneasily, the
simplicity of the moment passes, and
time flows
like a snapped twig on the current under the bridge.

I am whole inside. I speak a language
of distance and perspective, though I have
no words to explain why my bones grow cold.

I can run away, emptied of secrets,
utter my life in words no one else

understands, or sit in the corner with
my mouth shut.

I am beyond name and form,
stillness and movement together,
and when I see God I will be very small.
It is a confession I am making here:
I am asleep with no sense of time
And mumble quietly that the moment of waking is at hand.
The flow has ceased. Winter is coming again.
A cold wind whistles across the bridge.
A thin sheet of ice covers my face.

17.
The yard filled with smoke and then
the rooms of her house. I go outside.
Time slows, the horizon lifts.
The trees are indistinct black smudges
against the enveloping gray.

I close my eyes, feel my way inside
with the fingers of my hand. Life is
ordinary again. She sits in the corner
weeping but does not see me,
pale as old bones in gray smoke and dry light.

I lay my head on my arms. Night filters
through the window: embers of trees and
burned grass without substance or form in the distance.
The future invades my mouth, quivers
like the empty smell of smoke in the room.

There was a long silence. She says she is
a drop of water, a colorless bird, a piece of
glass, a cry in the dark, flesh of my own flesh,
and asks me to give her my fingers, one each day,
and let her stretch her life across to the far shore.

I will never be warm, I think, I will never be
warm, the thought coming and going like a wild
piercing of blood and earth, a sudden stirring of
life in the womb. In an instant I am gone
and in another I am back again, facing the wall.

18.
There is a smell of wet ashes in the air. I
cross to the window. It is nearly dark.

The world outside is blackened with burning,
moonlight and briny ice. Today is the day.

I am standing by the river, waiting for someone
to show me the way across. I am truth without
flesh.

The month is gone and the day. A woman's
cycle. I am standing by the window. It is
nearly dark.

There is no one here. I am already across the water and
home. I was bowed under the weight of the day.
The blur of a nervous river broods in my eye.

I kept my vigil for a day and night. It was nearly
dark. I returned to the riverbed. The flames flow
from me.

They burn the thought of something, of water that stands and
runs. Before this longing, the flames in one small fire, the eyes
vague.

I have fallen and she catches me. Tense, resistant,
hard. Now there is nothing to hold her. After a while I
was still.

The smoke dissolved and the heavens opened and the light
burns down penetrating and sharp. My voice tastes like wet ashes.

I yield to this contagion. The ghosts are gone. It is nearly dark.
Today is the day.
They fall and are washed away before they cross. I howl at the moon.

19.
All things are possible at the same time
everything from all sides
and nothing needs to be done to contain them.
 I have seen all things.
I have witnessed nothing.
I have been around every
corner.
I have been inside every wall.
I have failed in everything, in
nothing. I have returned from
everywhere,
from nowhere.
I have loved everyone, and
hated. I have seen my face in all
faces. I look at life passing
by. I am blind and deaf.
I see and hear everything.
I wait for what I do not know.
I am beginning to know myself.
I divide what I know, everything that exists,
exists. I am now and everything I never will be.
I am living right now.
I walk by, everything's hidden in the night that
remains. I lie down in the grass.
I am the landscape, the sky and
air. I think about nothing.
I speak I stop hearing. I write.
I forget myself.
I am the bridge, I am the sky, the first and final
star. I pick the black blossoms stirring my wings.

I am naked and plunge into the
water.
I feel the incandescent edges of the
world.

20.
Below the bridge
the water knows my name

its delicate
hesitations drained dry
as seasons
drift and disappear

cold winter salt
and flesh
and the river falls
running down and
standing still
against the panes of
the wind

invisible at night
splashing the lunar sky its
glide breaking
the erratic ice beneath the bridge

between the surface
and the slate-colored bottom
the shapes that cannot be seen
fresh weavings
of earth and air
over the snow at night
and the ghosts of the heart
in the ripening light.

Nocturne

1.
after Nijolė Miliauskaitė.

I know a place near the remains
of the detention camp where
when you brush your foot
across the sand the sand moans
sadly as if weeping

sometimes
a woman appears there, dressed in black
with eyes emptied of tears

wind carries her across the sand
like the shadow of a cloud

blows through her hair forever

2.
Night and a weightless moon
washed cold and white:
to lie naked in the sand,
hear the silence above the sunken tree,
rise and fall in the long moment,
slip through the slide and ache of your heart
and feel the slow pulse in the hand of God
as it touches your face in the lingering hour.

3.
It was the only way it could be known
the secret when the world began,
the centuries of dust, small things
sleeping forever in the earth,
the journey down the dry road,
the shattered glass of every

window, the withered white of a
single day.

And everything then seemed a single day.
the pain she felt, life on all fours, and later,
hands tied behind her back, her back to the wall,
a wrinkle in the sand, as the old men say,
dark collisions in the clouds, the votive
stone in the ground crying to come up
and out the way her soul might rise.

4.
Silence on your eyelids, clouds on the fragile face of the
day. Old roses in late September, petals falling and
falling. The night's slow song, the moon spread across the cold of
morning. The moment of turning, become another thing, as the
ground clears and the roots climb. Your grief that day was
something like this, your prayer rising to heaven, sand the
color of nothing
sifting through your hand as it clenches and unfolds.

5.
I stand by a low wall
indifferent to the stars
and watch all night.
She passes by like a thing
thrown into the air,
a little square
of fading black cloth.
In another world then
as now,
the lapse of time
as I look toward morning
and see salvation.
Overhead,
the light of oncoming
rain, the sky dense and
close.

The Only Thing the World Has Given Me to Keep

Nothing remains beneath the surface,
elemental things unraveling
in an elemental world.
I am willing to go along,
to accept that every living thing
is under siege,
bent to the changing light,
that the unmistakable cadences of every sound
in the world are a defiance of circumstance and death,
the one truth I know on this late autumn night.
I post no barrier between them.
I am high and low in this flying world,
a single continuum of earth and air,
brooding under water, over deserted sky.
I meet myself when the great wheel spins,
dressed in white,
stretched on the floor.
I open the one door I am not allowed to enter.
I give away the only thing
the world has given me to keep.

What the River Gathers

Magical lives, the mournful pace of a vanished world
no matter how dry the weather,
the night cold and still,
everything separate and distinct
along the side of the road,
no middle ground to disperse or preserve.
I watched women dressed in white swim silently in the pools of
the river,
floating softly in a blue haze
that weaved among the spider webs in the trees and rocks
caught and brittle on the banks.
I lift my arms like a white something,
skim the waters with unfamiliar birds.
Watch as the river gathers all that is left.
The river gathers the women and me.

Whittling the Root

Reason is not ambiance,
no miraculous increase that spills
across an unknown center,
the provisional point
inclined in no set direction
from some luminous core.
Things, instead, dim,
the precise and the absolute
—a precipitation of form that tilts time away
and overwhelms the natural and the useful.
There are a thousand close variables,
and tonight as fire splits the sky
and chaos knocks against the last closed window of the house,
I renounce the blindness of the world,
row myself across that dark final river
with the one hand that still functions,
whittle the changing root.

The Word

The word she hurled at me in the kitchen was a nail
driven through my hand
into the polished wood
of the table.
I can no longer leave this small room.
I accept the limitations of my destiny,
express no regrets, voice no complaints.
I fix my gaze on the glass of the window,
watch the whole scene repeat itself
as the light outside changes
to the color of gray rags.
She tries to pull it out each night
as I sleep bent across the table,
but the nail holds, it holds.

At the Sanctuary

The bird's feathers are sharp as razor points
Jabbed in every direction at once.

Facing West

It did not take us long to get there,
suddenly transparent as we face west.
The time before unexpectedly
became the time after.
The present changed too, unnoticed,
and we knew things must be hidden somewhere,
in the widening scope of disorder,
the abandonment of the uncertain bottom,
the rising and falling of the boards of the bridge.
The late sun sinks red as fire in the west;
the tide washes across the beach, its slow movements crimson
on the surface of the sand;
in the distance, out past the curve of the bay,
a ship emerges from the mist.

Brushing Away the Ink of Time

The hunger of the air,
the inner light of each visible thing,
the separation of black and white
on the wings of dead wrens.
Dawn returns, configurations
of interests and vows.
He no longer cares how far he wanders.
He is weightless on the old bridge.
His body rises as it falls,
conceives each distance, climbs every descent.
The circle drives each circle, each stone the next stone,
each hour the one before and then the next.
He brushes away the ink of time.
He can see the white sun rising in the west.

Genesis

The sky was the textures of an old gray dog.
The smells of the street, the noise frightening,
the threat deadly, incapacitating,
from heel to skull.
Even the living may not have a chance.
It had been dark for some time, smoke hollowing the horizon and
prowling the streets,
the gray spiders of ice gathering on all the windows and doors.
The snow bleeds on the bird's wing,
rough to the touch, stains the land red.
It is the truth that interrupts the answer.
The dust in my eye sets the dog loose,
nothing becoming nothing in a loud retort.
Pity the sky, the fallen roots.
Pity yourself and me.

The Ruins of the White City

The woman holds the bell
in her dark hand,
the death of the world
rusted as a beggar's cup.
There is a face in the glass in the wall,
a man with a stone in his hand
moving closer to the center of the light.
The earth blurs.
The moon drowns in the furrows of the river.
The crow hobbles the air,
alights in the ruins of the white city.

The Revenant's Prayer

I would return to summer light,
I would let the long rows of open doors not fade again,
 the yards rocking gently with wind,
birds flying past in endless flocks
and the willows slowly moving.
I would return to summer light,
would let gold and vermilion and shades of green
pour down across the wide horizon
to a glory overhead.
I would return to summer light,
would let the grace of water rise,
the air become the morning, coveting the earth,
a blue burning splendor of spirits and wings.
I would return, would rest in solitary places,
beyond the break in the trees,
beyond the easy breath of air,
where words are unfinished
and the echoes of my voice are a cry of love.
I would live all this again, and again,
would become eternal and whole in a silver light,
would turn it all once again, as I wait to be reborn,
into something reckless and endless and beautiful.

White Birds Fly By

He remembers walking down a path at the far end of the garden,
light twittering like a dying sparrow in soft wood,
the air leaning on vanishing roots, fog whirling slowly away
through clumps of dried grass and touching red blossoms.
He has learned to stand quietly as the light cries out
and stood there for a moment, for two,
as the crest broke and farther down, soft and clear, the green
sweep of bushes and birds tilted back into sunlight.
This is the slow change.
This is the body's perpetual beginning and end,
the reality of walking in the woods alone, in the curve and density
of unimaginable meaning beneath his feet, above his head.
Today, as the wind grows old, he closes his eyes
and sees the thing we feel in the evening nesting at its source.
White birds fly by. The world releases its forms. Time tips slowly
away on the other side of the sun.

Lost Plans

He planned to arrive in late spring, when children played on
sidewalks according to their own rules
and people sat along the walls in lawn chairs and on benches,
an unforced heartiness in their voices as they called to one another
across the street, gathering together defenseless in the sun.
A silent woman will walk beside him, thinking about her children,
knowing how to bear love.
His hand will touch her dark hair, a light wind will flutter off the
rooftops, lift the hem of her dress.

Snow Comes Sometimes Like a Quick Errand

He drove a dark red pickup truck with a bottle of Thunderbird
tawny port under the driver's seat.
His mother was swollen and yellow as that bottle when she died,
hair fine as feathers, voice quaking across the dim border of her room.
and he laughed without needing to apologize, to her or anyone else
for anything,
finished up whatever work he could find, put ketchup on his bread
before burying her
and threw an empty bottle of wine into the hole where they put her.
Snow came like a quick errand. He didn't bother with a coat.

Trimming the Lace

Her mind went blank, couldn't remember the names of all the
saints in all the congregations
that prayed for the dying and the dead.
Day was an opaque stone, fingers stained red, her arm bleeding, the
night insatiate. And so she prays: Blessèd is food, blessed is sleep,
blessèd is death, blessèd is the sand of the world, blessèd is the
dream of love and lost cities, blessed the turret of the grave, blessèd
the blazing plain. She trims the lace from around her wrist, sees the
hole that widens in the back of her yard.

The Things of the Eye

My eye is a flower shut tight at the center of a closed circle.
I sit on the bus by the window beside a woman who smells like
falling rain.
She talks quietly.
I hear the landscape of rain,
the hiss of lamps on street corners dimmed by rain,
the chiming of bells and dreams of glory,
the melody of expectation and promise full of movements
and pauses enlivened
and animated by rain.
My eye is an insect on her lithe, white thigh.
As it moves, I know that I know women, and how women are like rain.

From the Direction of the Door

after her mother died, she would call to tell me she wanted to sit
down on the floor,
in the middle of her room, with the lights turned off, to be where
she knew no one and no one knew her,
where no one wanted anything from her and she took nothing
in return,
to move at last through the unopened door and past the dark stair.
The night she died was abrupt and warm, midnight lifting up
and down the hall, something else, more urgent, coming from the
direction of the door.

Faltering On the Edge of the Future

About a mile and a half away, down along the banks of the brown
river, faltering on the edge of the future,
a distant barking of dogs hangs strangled in shadows and clouds.
He didn't know if he felt grief or love then and couldn't pretend
he heard something else slouching past the stone bench outside the
house and disappearing into thin air overnight, banished
forever from heaven.
Flesh of my flesh, cry of my cry, he mutters; the forgotten scars wake
to new leaves, shine mysterious and low in the window.

After the Waking of the World

The shaft of light on the path in the rain-soaked woods
brings the promise of day low on the horizon,
the trees' fiery shade, of hickory and ash,
a contemplation of the first waking of the world, of something from
nothing untethered at last.
Shadows play across her face.
The note sounds from far away.
She can see the endless wild uprush of white across the edge of the sky,
the infinite austerity of the stars waning to a pale flare of rusted knives.

The Indecisive Thing

He watched it pass the familiar chair, mysterious and sweet,
as a cold February day rattled the windows and gripped the front door.
He is up before the sun starts to warm the kitchen, rattling weak
as a lost love testing the horizon. His eye breaks tentatively to
the textures of gray light, picks time's bones apart as the harmless
gather in the unlighted rooms at the front of the house.
He tries to make himself small, radiate with a constant light that
dampens the black spaces on the walls,
then moves to perfection in the lines of the chair. he accepts his
end, and his final beginning,
the quick shiver when the wall grows cold, the unsteady night and
the time to come.
And then morning, the indecisive thing.

Calling Back the Light in the Mirror

He keeps a kerosene lamp burning by the window all night, its
flames a signal to keep away
the desolation and the cold that leaks through the shutters
on the landward side and worries the clapboards when heavy rain falls.
The light at last dusts the doorway, climbs up the painted walls of
the room
where she slept on the unmade bed, a sketch of pale colors opening,
breathing.
Outside, the wind squats in the eaves,
staggers in a tangle of roots.
He longs for the hour when the last lie grinds
through less than half the night,
when he shifts in bed and their eyes meet for a moment suddenly
in the mirror and then turn away, each of them staring, with a
snatch of breath, past the dimming lamp, across the empty sky.

With My Dying Brother
In memoriam A.P.Z. (1953–2018)

Some people are not helped at all, some people miss the whole
morning after the bus has come and gone ,
nothing close at hand.
He sits in the same chair in the same spot, reflecting a further
decline each night
nothing struggling to the fore, nothing possible to seize the past day.
Sometimes, when he can, he bends over his plate, staggers his words
to disbelief and mumbled disgust. All this so lightly wrought,
the dark grace of the vulnerable and dead.

The Light Said Nothing

He is surrounded by an odd light. The fires of August
change the landscape, trees burned to the shapes of grief,
smoke rising to an unbroken floor of clouds that bring no rain.
The uplands merge to patterns of belief,
the spokes of the world revolving to the enormous night beyond.
For a moment, then, we have a glimpse of ourselves, the mystery of
being between horizons, eternity a thin smoldering in dust
and dark patches on cold sand. We are a strange beauty. The world
 is empty as a shell, its edges wet and dark.
There was a light at the end of the long bridge.
The light said nothing.

Purposeful Pause

The illusion is set off by an extraordinary thing,
one wing tied behind his back.
Neither is afraid of the other, coal smoke scrubbing the horizon,
determined as stone, and the grass carved hard as brown marble.
A sign appeared suddenly on the roadside, urging salvation and
flattening the long complaints. He began to feel cold, his first
thought of shipwrecks and saved men.
It was a strange forgiving grace.
It was the salt-white emblem of redemption.
Dark water breaks the ice.
Life pauses for a moment in mid-flight.

Trapped Halfway Down the Hall

Time is the weight of cold silver, coil within coil trapped
at the bottom of the stairs.
The filaments of old bulbs, crooked with cold, crouch over wires
and boxes in the hallway. Outside, dry weeds sink in a black trunk.
Time is thistle and blood, labored hands that forget the truth of a
bitter embrace.
We are wayward things, elbows at our sides, devoured memories
fumbling down hallways to cloistered back rooms drawn with
faded paint, hiding cracks on the walls, our lives tied in a cart near
the pale trap.
We are wayward things, and the dead are nothing.
Someday I have to die and become nothing. But not now. Not now.

Epistemology

Somebody opens a window on the first great chill of fall
and in an unexpected moment of quiet he hears the infinite languor
of the world out past the gray horizon,
wayward birds roweled above a reddened sea,
dreams of old flowers as stars rain blind,
sleep spreading across the blank hush of the moon, wood darkening
to the vague voices of a yellow heart,
intractable edges of stained glass in arms as they fall,
murmurs of lost cities whipping the dark,
the arc of a needle scratching.
The world rolls on, love for love, riveting that other shore.
He records the tethered graces of this lengthening night—
time a drop of water suspended on a spider's web that trembles
forever in a trace of air or dries in the blink of a spider's eye.

When Something Calls

The gray sidewalk on the closed side street runs past a house of
rented rooms
where he sits in the dark by the window on the third floor drinking
whiskey and water,
thinking about things everyone else he knew had long since
forgotten.
An old newspaper is blown by a gust of wind across the street,
wraps around the foot of a statue
of three horses nothing but skin and bones, blood long gone back
to the river below.
He sits looking out, not sure how much had changed in the street,
in the empty yards and flat-roofed warehouses in the distance,
confidence and sorrow both marking the lines of his face.
He lights a cigarette, blows smoke in frail gray drifts
through the open window.
Something calls to him from the hall, gathering the strength to
walk home, trying to get back to where he ought to have been.
Anyone might wonder what that was.
He wondered, too.

Wind After Winter Rain

After two days of bitter cold and rain,
the wind changed in the night.
It has a way of coming suddenly to an end, adjusting itself,
then coming back to its own
beginning, driven in and out by winter rain as morning drifts to
its blind conclusions and the resistance of afternoon wears down at
last to night.
He's tired of this today, tired of the intricacies of chance that push
away human intention
and purposeful cause, of the dream or the ending of the dream
dancing like a jagged line in the corner of his eye.
He longs for some human design to take root
and work across the lost horizon,
wants to shape the world to suit his own purposes, to rust and
smoke and strange water. He closes his eyes for a moment and listens.
He leans into his own darkness. He will go east when he wants and
walk along the sea.

Winter's End

The road climbed up the long hill,
past the flock of crows on the flats
seizing what they could from the marsh
in the morning.
Winter brings necessity, somber wings beating the air above the
breakers, moving like slow smoke
through cuts and valleys in the dunes
in search of things washed up by the sea.
There is a blueness in the air, a coldness.
Black shapes turn and take to wing.

Through a Window Darkened By Night

He is alone once again and turns
to the photograph at the top of the page.
There, a thin woman with a sad smile and short brown hair holds
her hat in her hand and looks in the direction of someone just out
of focus, thinking about something that happened in her old life,
perhaps, or drawing on some private wisdom or intimate sense
about them both
that rested loosely like an arm on the railing of the porch.
A willow weaved its boughs just beyond the corner of the house
and a drab small child peeked out from behind the angular stairs.
The mortal solace of a moment plain and fixed from this distance in
time. The body taking on life once more, growing sharper and lighter,
and then swiftly gone as the sky drops clear and the dark clouds over.
He is alone, too, when he turns the last page.

At the Table in an Empty House

The air seemed to grow thick and heavy
without explanation and they held out no hope,
could not tell us the difference between that time and now.
She could not remember clearly who had moved on
and who had stayed,
could not imagine finding it all in the state it was in today—the
ground hard, stones everywhere, the apprehensions of old words as
redeeming as a bad dream
or short and blasting as a general alert.
She would find herself separated in the whole arrangement,

sensible as sitting at the table of an abandoned house,
believing in divine tricks and magic doors opening and closing
above the cold stars.
The light from outside illuminates another view, the bare floor that
parries the darkness, and, just past the screen door, the shallow mud.

Son of a Pale God

He grew flowers in the winter in the hothouse window at the end
of the kitchen,
orchids and hyacinths
interspersed with small shrubs of rosemary and pots of basil,
thin stalks of cilantro with white blossoms,
long stems of dill going to seed,
coriander and parsley and thyme.
He wasn't interested in his neighbors or the general news, wore
blue latex gloves to protect the plants from his own drilled touch,
his strokes of misfortune and errors in judgment—
the raw face of morning as it toggled his skin.
The presence of life sustains life, he would say, the rituals of each
day a call to a pale god to linger in the room among the flowers.
There were times, on the threshold of spring, when he tried to
open the unopenable door.

Gray Mask

He imitates the world, huddles in a small room painted red,
the door near the farthest window stiff and white as a starched
collar. Everywhere else seems strange to him, ghosts of dust and
light recalled in unsent letters,
etched in the silence of stones and walls.
Persistent things nest in a corner of his eye:
a patch of moonlight on the ceiling
crying out in the night, flesh dissolving to water
that fills a roadside ditch,
God's hands buried in black snow.
The clock in the room is striking, the hour unclear.
He hears a soft quick step and somewhere in the east ,
a world away, time spins on its point, the gray mask rises.

Following My Own Footprints

There are stars, and to the west Antares hangs above a landscape
where every vibration is stilled,
save for the sound of waves breaking and the faint echo of the moon,
now two days full, spilling across the sand.
A dark crust of burned moss drops
from the rocks into the water,
a thin unity along the headlands more than an easy failure or whirl.
The wind is steady and high and the land falls to clear transitions,
dry wings abandoned and bodiless as the year comes to a dead rest.
Don't ask me to ask the roots to tell me how branches fill the empty
places
with inexpressible light, how the dips and rises of the world are a
miraculous increase, radiance entangling the core,
how reality's cold waters overspill the black mountains,
as I watch my footprints disappearing at the edge of the sea.
I don't know what else there is.

Early Warnings

They warn you when you start out to do this,
astonished to find yourself alive,
beyond the secrets of the moon and the white hands of the sea.
No trace or vestige of triumph, no place and no reproof.
The forgotten scars of the ditch burn their way to wires, one of
the many shadows where spiders root and weep. You roll down the
hill, abandoned and bewildered.
You move so slowly that you do not move.

At the Door of My House

I watched the birds pass above the tree line
in fearless intervals, low just above the tops
of the maples and oaks
and dark against clouds
smoking
along the lower edge of the sky.
Shadows gathered in the cuts of the visible horizon
and there was a tang in the air.
Something was happening, perhaps different than what happened
before,
and I could not hear what you said, your faced pressed against my
back, your hands and the earth smelling of old leaves and dust.
The moon dropped a thin shaft of light on the dried rosebushes.
The birds scattered from the trees and squatted near the door in a
rough half circle, facing in and out, in and out, shuffling a dance.
You wept and turned away. The whole day there went dark.

Hearing Voices

She was rocking on the edge of her future,
the ceiling of the bedroom white and high,
the windows indistinct as faded letters
in the corners of the walls.
The sweet wind blew soft as her ecstatic moan across the corners
of her bed.
The door was swinging back and forth in the front hall,
making a sound so small that she didn't notice when it stopped.
She picked up the suitcase, carried it downstairs,
and laid it open on the floor.
She was tired of all this irrelevance, promised herself to do
whatever she could.
This is what she bargained for. This is how the tide comes across
the square.
This is why the accusation fails again and falls. Shadows clouded
her way across the room.
When she turned, she heard voices.

Hand Against Hand at the End of the World

The Finnish girls tug on loose cloth,
their white hands exhausted.
The one on the right taps her foot softly out of rhythm,
the one on the left hums under a red scarf.
There is someone else in the room, standing at the window,
gazing into a starry sky.
There is the sudden sound of a body hitting the earth.
Ukko stumbles through the reeds, back and forth, swift, ephemeral,
the rumor of his ghost a rush of breath, the crack of bone that
cannot be mended.
The girls turn: the brush of hand against hand at the end of the world.

Making No Sound

It all ends soon enough. The first days become the last.
The year is a pile of dry bones scattered near a low brown fence,
the trailing edge of a broken wing dragging on the water.
For her the world turned white once more, her blind eye closing in
the high room.
Her life is a crooked line written on the sidewalk in pale chalk
before rain.
The lost patterns of death wear away the hours, loosen the pale
wonders of the sky: faded, far away, dissolved, forgotten.
You roll down the hill, abandoned and bewildered.
Your voice bends, makes no sound.

The Ashes of Dead Stars

What she said was not a plea, though the uncertainty in her voice
surprised him as he suddenly turned
toward her, startled her to breathe again as the hour finally passed.
Her red dress fluttered by the kitchen window, in late afternoon
at the edge of the small town where the plain sky grows so blue
and a good woman's prayers,
in the anonymity of her room,
might reach for heaven.
There was no loneliness like hers, she murmured .
With each step she took to close the curtains she kicked the ashes
of dead stars.

In a Blue Crucible

The mingling I speak of may take place again.
He hopes this is the last truth,
deeper than any memory
deeper than any sense of constancy or change.
When she left him in the mirrored room, with a look infinitely sad,
dark hair outlined
by her linen dress, he saw himself grow suddenly transparent
until there was nothing of him
in any mirror or dark glass, imperfection hidden in the dulls and
echoes of a more permanent night.
Let those shadows sleep and turn to dust.
Let our love play us across the room, he whispers.
The hesitant lie persists. The mirror swings like a crucible in blue.

About the Author

Jonas Zdanys is the author of fifty-six other books. They include collections of his poetry written in English or in Lithuanian and volumes of his translations into English of Lithuanian poetry and fiction. He is also editor of several anthologies, among them collections of found poetry, epistolary poetry, and, most recently, contemporary surrealist and magical realist poetry. He serves currently as Poet in Residence and Professor Emeritus of English at Sacred Heart University.